Unflappable Women

Also By Esther Buffler

Poetry:
String of Beads
Grandmother's Quilt
Nine Children

Juveniles:
Mary
Rodrigo and Rosalita
The Friends

Plays:
Rodrigo and Rosalita (adaptation)

Unflappable Women
By Esther Buffler
Cover Illustration By Patricia Buffler

Esther Buffler (signature)

The Golden Quill Press
Manchester Center, Vermont
Publishers Since 1902

©Esther Buffler 1994
Library of Congress Catalog
Card Number 94-07987

I.S.B.N. 0-8233-0496-5

Printed in the United States of America

The Unflappable Poet

*L*ife abundant and joy strung in the rafters is what I find in the poetry of Esther Buffler, who not only addresses life and real people, but memorializes, enhances, and endows her topics, her people, our world with a steady, loving vision and a deft touch of expression. She is the unflappable poet, whose calm energy and radiance generates hope and happiness in us all.
*-- Morris Edelson, Houston Quixote Press/
Art Institute of Houston*

*E*sther Buffler's voice is unmistakable. Readers who can only encounter her words on the page will miss the rare experience of hearing her imbue those words with the music and inflections of the performer that she is. Still, the texts carry the heart and substance of her art,

In this fourth poetry collection, Buffler celebrates the vitality of the strong, influential and unsung women in her life. She gives them both a renewed identity and a contemporary platform for their issues and ideas, dreams, disappointments and legacies.

Esther Buffler came late to poetry after successive careers as wife, mother, radio personality, art dealer, playwright and professional stage actor. Her idiosyncratic style and profound compassion combine to produce work that is utterly original. She sports a stunning array of hats, each one stylish and perfectly her own.

--Marie Harris

*E*sther Buffler was born in Pennsylvania, trained in theatre, married a professor of architecture and spent most of her married life in the world of academe in Austin, Texas.

Widowed at a young age, she established a new life for herself and her two sons in New York where she returned to her earlier field of the theatre. She worked on the legitimate stage, radio, television and film. Eventually, she retired from New York City to Portsmouth, New Hampshire.

It was here that her career as a poet flowered. She was published in journals and in the books, *String of Beads*, *Grandmother's Quilt* and *Nine Children.*. Esther Buffler has served in the poetry program of Artists in the Schools; children's poetry teaching program of the Prescott Park Arts Festival; on the professional staff of the Star Island Conference on the Arts at the Isles of Shoals where she conducted poetry seminars; at the Derry, New Hampshire Robert Frost celebratory year introducing grade school children to Frost and his poetry and as consultant and facilitator of children's poetic creativity in a number of public schools.

To the courage of women --
and in memory of my mother, Mary,
and my grandmothers, Maria and Araminta

Author's Note:

Gratitude expressed to all who have listened, published and shared in my work. I appreciated the hours of critique expressed by poets of Skimmilk Farm, Brentwood, New Hampshire. My family's loyalty and love means much in my life; also, bracing friendships, so many that would fill the page. They stay ever close to me. Special thanks to Jim Halpin and Alan Anderson of The Great Bay National Wildlife Refuge, Newington, NH for allowing me an early observation of 'what's ahead' for the Refuge. Kudos are due to teachers of Delta Kappa Gamma Society International, Gamma Chapter, New Hampshire for bestowing upon me an honorary membership for writing an epic poem in recognition of a courageous early American teacher (my mother).

Contents

Part One - Unflappable Women

Mary Anders Rogers, An American Story	2
Marlene	13
The Day I Broke The Lampshade	14
April	21
Violeta	24
Winter Closes In	25

Part Two - On The Go

A Visit To The Big Apple: Thanksgiving	28
Crosstown	29
Museum Fever	32
Opening Night Broadway	33
Seduction	34
In A Heap On The Floor Of A Bloomingdale's Elevator	35
Friends	37
Penn Station	40
Still Life 1990	41
Reawakened November One, 1991	42
Vienna	43
Is	45
The Pummerin Bell	46
New Orleans	48
Mother's Breakfast	49

Beaux Arts	50
A Burning Thorn	51
Old Cemetery	52
The Garden District	53
Berkeley	55
Chicle Tree, Guatemala	57
Dialogue	58

Part Three - New England

Portsmouth Sunday	62
Hurricane Rose	63
O Dear God	64
Seasons	65
Wildflowers	66
Prescription	67
Ace	68
Day Lilies	69
Jolted	70
The Cricket Call	76
Breaking The Tomb Of Winter	77
Newmarket Public Library	78
Forest Hill Farm	79
A Summer's Wreath	81

Part Four - A Jugful Of Other Poems

Jugful	84
A Beatitude	85
Gifts	86

Writer And A Fish	87
fly ash	88
Lenny Tree	89
Visitation	90
Daylight Saving	91
In A Disfigured World	92
A Cadence	93
Elizabeth Alexandria Booth Wold	94
Sweet Death Houses	95
Last Rites	98
Elegy For Robert Jebb	99
...the praying man	100
Morning	101
Texas Afternoon	102
Elizabeth	103
A Canvas	104
Lovers	105
Legs	106
Time Waits Out Time	107
The Narcissus Eye	108
Home Free	109
Friendship	110

Part One
Unflappable Women

Mary Anders Rogers
1879-1971
An American Story

*B*orn of farm families, rich
in land, love and work,
a wild middle child
running the fields,
climbing the woods,
jumping the mows,
bunching watercress,
watching the cattle copulate
in the barnyard,
snatching pet George
blacksnake by the back of its head,
curious, fearless.
She rubbed the fuzz off the orchard's ripe peach and
bit into its sweetness.

Flushed out, sensing others ...
<u>medicine, that's it!</u>
She listened at the parlor door:
Uncle doctor Jim spoke to her father;
<u>Hiram, she will never be accepted
in my profession, she's a woman,
let her teach.</u>

She blushed, felt unhinged.
Obeyed.

Record:
first Pennsylvania State Normal School,
Millersville, class of 1900;

honors graduate, class reciter.
First job teacher, one-room rural school,
first through eight grades.
Pay: eighty dollars a month.
Heat, round-bellied woodstove,
stoked by farmer's son, one dollar
per week paid by her.

Her man. First and only.
She found him at a string game party:
quick touching hands in the unwind;
first prize, necktie and linen handtowel!

Early dew (five years engagement).
Marriage. June wedding on the lawn...
roses, more roses and the sweet mock orange,
hands to shake and bride to kiss...
and off to Niagara Falls!

5 a.m. Cock crows. The farmer's wife,
her gorgeous long brown hair fixed in a knot
which always looked as it might fall down,
she cooks, sweeps up, plants and hoes
the truck patch, mends, tends the chickens
and turns the churn.

Heavy hay harvest, she helped with barn work.
Sweat poured as she stripped udders for that
last squirt from the Holsteins.
Haywagons piled with mounds of sweet glory,
pulled up onto the barnbridge and into the
barn floor with a satisfied bump! A huge
spiked iron fork was thrust into hand of hay;
this was fastened by ropes to a pulley
on a wooden plank; this to the harness of a team
of two horses. She held tight their reins
and hollered <u>yyyeeeeeeeup go!</u>

As team they forged up the barn hill;
the forked hay lifted to the top of the barn
where it connected to tracks, flew wildly
to the mows and dropped airily down. Men
leveled it! She and the horses trooped wearily
down the hill as the fork returned to reload.
Days sighed to an end; the tedder and hayrake
settled in for dust of winter.
Her bright Schwenkfelder sunbonnet folded
in to the drawer in season.

Suppertime carried its special melody,
and she the conductor of pots and pans.
Lids of the big iron stove came crashing
off like cymbals! Quick fire was started
with dry corncobs spitting pizzicati.
She sat in her rocking chair peeling potatoes,
dropping them one by one into cold water
like the plunk-plunk from a cello!
Corn to be husked, string beans to be snipped,
pickled beets, pie and milk brought from the cellar,
coffee by tablespoon measured into large
blue enameled coffee pot (let it fume up but not
boil over, quick with the eggshell)!
Father followed by hired-hands washed up at the
outside pump. Over a bench in the mirror;
combed, smiled, bowed they entered the dining room.
No small talk, just ate. Ate. We sat together
at the round table. She looked amused, seemed
to be waiting. The hands satisfied, left.

Suddenly it was if the night breeze swept away
the day. Our lives changed. She put a fresh
cover on the dining room table and brought in our
large coal oil lamp. She always had handy
two or three books. Father unfolded his newspaper.
O glory of Goodrich Silvertone orchestra! Brother

and I snatched earphones hanging next to our homemade
oatmeal-box cat's whisker radio. Very faint
but there it was ...

Father's chair came down with a bang to the floor
from its usual leaning position! <u>Read this Mother,</u>
handing her the newspaper. We pulled off our
earphones. She read:

> <u>New district school building opens</u>
> <u>in the fall. Teachers needed.</u>
> <u>Application ...</u>

Her eyes came up. Well?
Did she need to ask.
<u>yes, Yes, YES, you must,</u>
<u>yes, Yes, YES, you must,</u>
we hollered.

In starched red and white gingham dress
father drove her to the School Board meeting
in our first car, a worn second-hand Saxon.
Two hours later they were home. Confidence
showing in her straight shoulders she held high
the signed letter of her appointment:
> <u>Principal and sixth grade teacher</u>
> <u>to lead district school in new era</u>
> <u>of teaching. Vote of Board unanimous.</u>

We were not a kissing family. I cried, patted
her lap. Brother sat still. Father touched
her hair.

Something new opened into our family. Happiness
rolled in. We talked more together, did more
things: train connecting in New York for boatride
up the Hudson; a new long brown wool coat for her

and a Backhawk bike for me! A monthly trip
to Philadelphia (Strawbridge & Clothier charge)
and always a visit to Museum & Art Gallery!
Brother at School of Industrial Art. Father
had a new second-hand car. And when the pond
froze, I pulled off the peg my old key skates!
Joe's dark head was gorgeous bending down fixing
them expertly to my worn shoes. We held hands
and skated under a winter's moon.

HEADLINES: 1932. Men need jobs! Women suspect.
Taking men's jobs! Married women stay at home,
give jobs to wage earners, the men! Local
School Board petitioned. Action considered.

The Times Herald flung on the front yard.
There it was:

> WOMEN TEACHERS FIRED
> Three married teachers dismissed.
> Salaries, $110-130 per month. No
> question as to their ability.
> Husbands can support them. Parents
> in uproar with protest!

A deep furrow on her soft brow appeared.
She gazed at me. I did not understand.
I felt squirrely and hot.

At home laughter fled.
Murmurings - then action!
A lawyer was hired,
the case went to court.
Her mien was heroic
standing before the jury.
Men and women. Atmosphere
tense. Reporters poised;

in from Philadelphia Evening
Bulletin! Judge's gavel:
verdict;
> ... teacher's ability
> unquestioned, but married,
> not self supporting, resignations
> required immediately . . .

It was over.
I did not see her cry.
Nor hear poundings of her heart.
I will never know her agony,
the dark nights of turned over
deepenings of soul. I was
humiliated in silly pride.
My bright, beautiful mother
had LOST!

Reality hit us. Her pay check
cut off, what about us?
She held firm. College based
scholarships for us, then
marriage.

A small farm up country came up
for sale. They looked over twenty
acres of glacial land snugged under
foothills of the Poconos. Just
a stage set? She took his arm.
<u>We can handle this, father, yes.</u>

Crops small: lived mostly on
what they raised and grew. Two
pigs, one cow, two horses, chickens.
Her truck patch a beauty! Huge
wooden bowls of dried corn, peas,
beans, sorted and tucked under

attic eaves. The shed held rows
of shining jars of ground cherry,
gooseberry, raspberry and blackberry
preserves. Jellies of currant, quince,
and too many apple and grape! Chow-chow
her prize along with beets, string beans,
corn and an abundance of tomatoes filled
the bottom shelves. Top shelves held
carefully picked seeds for next year's
crop, these in paper bags tied and marked.
In the root cellar: stone jar of vinegar,
bins of potatoes (white and sweet);
apples, onions, eggs in waterglass,
and a jug of homemade dandelion wine.
This brought up for special visitors,
was served in mother's small
cranberry glasses; the Reverend got a
second serving.

She was an outdoor person, carried
a sturdy tree limb for her walking stick;
spotted wild grasses, bark, gums, herbs
for the local black herbalist. <u>Look here,
Mr. White, sassafras ... pine gum... ginseng.</u>
They sat on the porch, rocked out a tune
together. Former students appeared up
the dirt road, sat on the porch, feet
on the bench; pumped water from the deep
well, chomped on her shoo-fly pie, coffee
cake; savored her special lemon sponge!
Her exuberance matched theirs.

<u>Let me show you what happened around here
last month!</u> She brought forth from the cell room
a mounted eight foot copperhead! <u>Killed
it with the sharp edge of a shovel...</u>

<u>takes a sharp edge you know.</u> She winked.
An aura of mystery, many people came to talk;
a storyteller, in character with nature
She wrote me, <u>I'm putting up my shingle!</u>

First startled winds of fall.
The ancient hop vine buds scratched
against the plumped out concord grapes.
The paper boy threw the Times Herald
with a <u>Hi, missus</u>... She raised a hand,
then settled down to read the news. She noted
the second page; small print, she adjusted her
glasses, read:
> <u>Upper county school to close.</u>
> <u>Men off to war. Teacher</u>
> <u>shortage.</u>

She rose slowly. Head up. It was
time to start supper. Instead
she went to the desk and carefully
removed those well-kept, brittle, more
than twenty years ago credentials,
and slid them into a fresh envelope.

After a hurried supper, sitting at the kitchen
table, she handed father the paper.
He read the first page... into the second...
paused, put it down. There eyes met.
> <u>I can drive you up the hill,</u>
> <u>whenever you're ready.</u>

Combed, bloused and skirted, oxfords
polished, she was ready!
Her 'knight in armor' tapped on the window.
He had been inspecting grain bins for the
government all day and was brushing off his hat,
<u>different farming now!</u> They drove off...
No words spoken. The Ford coupe bounced

down the road holding at bay the sunset.
At the top of the long hill sat the tidy
white house of the Board's president.
Father opened the car door. She stepped
forth. He nodded,
> I'll wait for you.

The all male School Board motioned to her.
They did not stand.
> Please be seated.

She smiled, sat down, handed her records
across the table to them.
The Board's president tightened:
> See that you were dismissed once?

> Yes, because I am a woman and married.
> All of you married?

Five men's heads came up in surprise.
As if answering a joke.
> Yah, our kids go here.

> Good! Wonderful!

All looked pleased. Her eyes steady
on them. They hitched suspenders, left
the room. She was not to hear their thoughts.
What were hers?

They reappeared.
> Well, Missus, looks like you got the job.

She rose.
> Thank you, gentlemen, you will
> be pleased with your decision.
> Goodnight.

Two aging people sat in an aged car.
Years ago they had sat close
on that first horse and buggy ride.
Again their bodies touched.
The night was golden. Home. They trod
over mowed grass toward their 18th century
stone farm house. Tiny "Hens & Chickens"
crevassed in a huge glacial boulder
shimmered with cups of dew. Hollyhocks
like ghostly dancers swayed to night tunes.
Flowers bunched as one looked at them
under a harvest moon.
The large handmade iron front door key
turned under her hand to embers in glow
from woodstove. Spits of fire shot forth.
> <u>Come mother, we'll climb the "wooden hill"
> to bed.</u>

Seven, eight years she learned from them.
Thought, taught, walked in stride with youth.
Her own children, grandchildren brought joy
with each visit to the farm like sweet hay
harvested. At her seventy-fifth birthday,
memorable as a wedding anniversary she
announced, <u>I'm not quitting but shall leave
my one-room school and give strength to
needed tutorials.</u>

Fine August morning. Breakfast over, her man
raised a hand to the sun. Horses needed to be
curried, bedded and fed. He entered the stall,
fell beneath the horse. Stroke. His grandson
carried him to the house. Death eased through
him. She knelt with a sob, eyes half-closed,

body close on his chest.

Burial. 'All gave nod'. There were tears.
I held her hand. She shook then steadied,
lips moving but no sound came... felt
like we were rehearsing a Shakespearian sonnet.

Months later I drove cross country from Texas
to take over. Up early one a.m., we sat chatting
over our usual oatmeal. Two widows. Renovations
to the house? She pushed back her chair. Brought
me up short: <u>I'm fine. I'm healing. You're young,
have presence. Things are much better for us women
...well, slowly. Theatre is your work. Go for it!
Are you serious,</u> I interrupted.
<u>Yes, don't ever let anyone tell you I'll not be happy
here alone... so many blessings, besides I prefer
my own ways...</u>

I left. We wrote each week. If the letter didn't
come through on time, she'd call the P.O.
At every break, I was on the bus, homeward bound.

Family, friends, helpers, former students,
all came to sit on the porch. She rocked
in tune with each new day ...<u>yes, yes I'm pushing
92 ...don't worry about me, the angels come to visit,
sometimes they feel quite near...</u>

The brown wren twittered and stroked a wing
to us at the windowpane. Tail raised, it jabbed
into a chunk of suet she had nailed to the ancient
grapevine. With a spirited look, she nodded
and reached for my hand.

Marlene

*When all networks flashed
news of her death, I wrote*

*B*ackstage she stood.
Tall, slim, beauty in planes
of face, arched arid eyebrows;
waiting, longing in full lust
for him, the star of our show.
Final curtain descended slowly,
then hit the stage with a <u>zump!</u>
He was young, proud, handsome,
cynical. A smile, and with bodily
rejection turned away, as to say,
<u>old one</u>. All of us saw it.
Disquieted, hastily, we left
to remove make-up . . . . . .

The Day I Broke The Lampshade

The 100-year-old lamp shade
lay shattered on the floor!

What was the intent of this happening?
Solely an accident? Picking up pieces,
did I fear obscene images of broken
cheek bones, ears askew, chips of teeth,
blood from a tattered pink rose?

Stalking through the bedroom
to the bureau where in a wreath stood
a picture. We looked upon one another.
Framed, on a creased fragile paper,
her last scripted words:

>   Sarah
>
>   We say if for an hour or for years;
>   We say it smiling, say it choked with tears;
>   We say it coldly, say it with a kiss;
>   and yet we have no other word than this. -
>   Good-bye.
>
>   Mrs. N.R. Rogers
>   Lower Merion
>
>   Feb. 5, 1884

Dead at forty.
Dead before I was born.

The chill of the day would not go away;
a dankness like descending to the casket-

room of a funeral parlour. I shuddered
imagining all those with stretch sly
smiles gently locked in shining satin.
Out loud, <u>not for me, it's the old lady
of Cork's black woolen shawl with fringe,
wood, the earth!</u>
But what about her? With cup of fresh tea,
settled in reverie, and like acid in stone
each word touched me. Her story had been
a din in the ear forever.

>Spirited youngster, quieted down
>now with mother gone, she was brought
>to America by father. He, a determined
>Scot, member of the wool Guild
>of Glasgow, took her by the arm, sailed
>for Philadelphia. He placed her in best
>school, Friends Select! Their Betsy Ross
>brick house could not hold all his friends.
>He drank. He also became the finest cutter-
>of cloth for the city's best dressed men.
>She was lost ... except for Hannah! In-
>separable at school, Hannah's family
>invited her to the country to visit.
>Deep in rolling Pennsylvania farmland
>her spirits bounced. She had missed
>the firth but this was comforting.
>Nathan was there, too! Horse and buggy
>clipping down the lane! Her gem-like hazel
>eyes, his gliding blue met! Marriage.
>She moved to the far County.

Let my father, her eldest son take up the story:

>There were seven of us. Each bumping into
>the other; chores galore. Mealtime a triumph;
>especially mashed potatoes done by a wooden

smasher; Sunday's stewed chicken (an old hen)
served with large dish of creamed onions;
stewed tomatoes laced with cubes of stale white
bread; bread and butter pickles (sought after
recipe); pumpkin pie made with eggs, pumpkin,
sugar, spices and no milk; hot turnip slaw!
Scrubbed in the big tub, dressed in best, ready
for night at the local Grange. We filled the falling-
top, buggy, and arrived for front seating to watch
her perform in skits she had put together, directed.
Not supposed to applaud, but we did. She sang, too.
Many times we prayed it wouldn't be quite so loud!
Harvest parties, we were the stars, handing out
pumpkins to all who came; hopefully they would vote
for Nathan, our father, who usually ran for County
Commissioner. Scary, the evenings a tramp would tap
at the kitchen door. She would fix him a plate,
take away his pipe and tobacco, hand me the lantern
as I showed him the barn, haymow for sleep.
Springtime; time for the old peddler to come?

My father lit his pipe. Shook his head, continued:

The peddler: late afternoon, one of us would spot
him coming clackety-clack down the pike in his old
black falling-top; whip urging on tired sway-back
gaited nag. All made beeline for the house.
From the window we watched, fascinated. With a swerve,
he pulled into our lane, tied up the horse; got out
with help of an ebony cane, pulling after him a huge,
heavy black case. Removed from his mouth a cud of chewing
tobacco, spit, tipped his worn black fedora at a rakish
angle, stroked his beard and limped toward the kitchen
door. Mother was waiting. <u>Well, welcome Mr. Isadore!</u>
She motioned us all into dining room to see better!
Our breathing trailed him as a song, smell from another
world. Magic as the black straps of his case loosened,

locks unsnapped and falling forth in rhythm a series
of shelves displaying a wondrous assortment! We didn't
ask, just pointed, longingly. Our mother nodded as Mr.
Isadore piled 'em up: suspenders, camphor liniment,
witch hazel, men's red and white handkerchiefs, pin-
cushion, toothbrushes, castile soap for hair washings,
pair ladies side-combs, packets of pins, needles,
buttons, spools of thread, white & black, and colored;
mousetraps, shoestrings, dress stuffs . . . so many things.
Each of us allowed to select a small thing. She then
picked out a bottle of lavender water. That meant she
was through. Mr. Isadore would fish around in the bottom
shelf, smile, present her with two small envelopes
of floral carnation sachet!
We lugged his heavy case across the grass,
put it in the wagon and waited: <u>the cane, Mr. Isadore!</u>
He bowed, fiddled with a hidden button on top
of the ebony stick and with a flourish pulled forth
a long, thin steel blade! We shouted! We clapped!
Waved him good-bye. Another few weeks, and time
for another event. Sarah's visit!

I bent over the fragments, gently picked up a porcelain
leaf. Looked at the framed note. Pulled up the blind
for more light. <u>Hello</u> . . . my father spoke, almost
a whisper:

> Sarah Cassidy! She came to sew, to love us,
> to love me. Sent from the city by her father,
> she brought each a shining gift, her self.
> Jokes, swapping stories from <u>across the waters:</u>
> recipes; laughter, fun, happiness . . . The sewing
> machine made merriment in a hum of music under
> the running beat of her feet on the treadle; new
> shirts and pants; women's duds; blouses & bows;
> skirts; aprons; latest fashions from the city.
> Mostly, her time alone with our mother; walks

over the meadow down to Stony Creek wading in
bare feet . . . screaming as leeches sucked their
blood! Nights settled in reading; Dickens, Hardy,
Thackeray, Keats. Between them, mother's treasured
wedding gift, the new tin lamp with porcelain
painted shade.

Derivation.
Was I creeping around in sentimentality?
Family lineage, the lamp, passed down, finally
landed with me; over mountains, valleys, rivers Hudson,
Delaware, Schuylkill, Mississippi!
The tin base bent, pulled back in shape. The porcelain
lamp shade, a wonder, perfect. Until today!
Old shade, old woman? My ninety-year old aunt's
shrill words taunting me fleeted back: <u>wait until
you're my age, but then all you seem to care about is books,
not housekeeping.</u>
Right you are, I thought. Then I felt her mood soften.
I knew what was coming. Heard my aunt say:

> Christmas Eve. Our cheeks were flushed,
> all day finishing up the baking, candy-
> making. I was prize-picker of shellbarks
> from our woods. Stockings had been washed,
> now hanging behind the stove to dry;
> sneaked in to taste the soft creams, jelly-
> centered, cooling in the cell-room; shelves
> lined with pies; mince, pumpkin, and favorite
> raisin! Our boys had cut big pine tree from far
> field; up, trimmed; the huge tinsel silver
> star at the tip-top looked out into the little-
> used-in winter parlour. Cold. Not much under
> the tree; each a something and handmade.
> It was the tree! I can still smell it!

Women kin, we wept. Did I feel rising from the shade's
fragments a coming together of lives piece by piece?
Let my aunt continue:

> Excited and tired. Our mother very quiet.
> Looking back, I now feel she must have known.
> Remember, the note she wrote to Sarah in springtime?
> She called each of us by name, drew us to her side,
> eye to eye, hard hug and a kiss. Sent us to bed.
>
> Must have been nearing morning ... streaks
> in the sky.
> Called, I toddled to her bedside. The others
> were there. They had been sent to the creek
> to break ice for her fever.
> Old Doctor Slifer was bent low over her.
> Our father held high the lamp.
> We knelt, crying, praying
> <u>open your eyes, open your eyes,</u>
> <u>please, Please.</u>
> She didn't.
> Our father spoke:
>
>> <u>Mother has flown away ...</u>
>> <u>like a snowbird, I guess ...</u>
>> <u>somehow, we'll manage.</u>
>> He looked at each of us.
>> Placed the lamp gently
>> on the bedside table.

The lamp still a visitor on the bedside table?
Restoration? Get on with it.
Find a craftsman worthy of the job.

Finally, the ten-times-ten years lamp shade
is glued together.
It rests in grace upon its base
at my bedside. Books, notes, papers piled ...
Those toady face chips in my mind
floated away, spelled themselves out ...

A dim, thin crack like a long stem
reaches in glow on a painted porcelain
wild rose.

April

*A*nd she came in on time,
awakened all to song.

High tides of the Piscataqua
swept under the ice floes;
breath of the wind was fierce;
tattered patches of snow like worn-
out sweaters appeared dirty
and ridden on the banks. Maine
side, the creaky rowboat, oars
angled, awaited. We sat bundled,
eared down, white scalloped hair
touching. Talkers we were squinting
at the sun. Morning news had been
bad. VIOLENCE.
Our voices caught the wind,
reminiscing... ...

> <u>I saw Bath burned.</u>
> <u>I saw Bristol bombed.</u>
> <u>Planet still reeks!</u>

Touch tone, I answered:
> Violence - like a white heat
> of cancer continues on. Blood
> from it keeps spilling.
> Think back. Think back
>
> as when those ten stripes
> to each naked back
> brings a cold chill

from winter, 1662, Dover Neck,
New Hampshire. Parson, people, friends
stood shivering on the Common.
The Piscataqua moved swiftly, snow
bit into faces. King's Magistrate's
warrant was read:

> ...you and every one of you
> are required in the King's Majesty's
> name to take these vagabond Quakers,
> Anna Coleman, Mary Tomkins, and Alice
> Ambrose, and make them fast to the
> cart's tail, and drawing the cart
> through your several towns, to whip
> them upon their naked backs...

'twas done. 'twas done.

> Anna: We hold to one another
>   sustained by Inner Light.
>
> Alice: Low to the ground am I, aged,
>   crooked and bent. A good kick
>   to his crotch should've sent!
> Mary: No. No. Only fearful they were
>   to disobey orders
>   from Massachusetts Bay.

Three towns beyond, through brutal weather,
rucked roads, mud, tender bodies raw,
the Constables saw them coming. All moved
in quiet steps of grace...
the women then released in peace.
In small boats, first to Maine, then back
to Dover Neck they came. Welcomed.
Undaunted, they found work, shared
friendships, brought wisdom, pleasure
to each day. Peace.

*

Red and purple streaked through the sky.
Our small boat now anchored at dock.
Climbing the bank, up the path by leaf
and rock, bright-eyed crocuses lifted
their heads as if to say; <u>bit by bit,</u>
<u>year by year</u>
<u>Life is an Absolute.</u>

Violeta

*l*ook at us now!
Millions - millions
of faces. Hear my voice
holding tight in banded
bones of Light in a small land

with the bridle from the
dark horse FEAR taken off

as we understand loving kindness
from the heart of a grandmother.

Winter Closes In
Sit And Try To Understand

Why the white winter cactus
blooms each year at Christmas?

A juxtaposition.
We breathe upon one another.

The two of us have a questioning;
will there be yet another year together?

December is my birthday month.
The bloom of the cactus is feathered
with red. Red is my color.

Part Two
On The Go

A Visit To The Big Apple: Thanksgiving, NYC 1993

being away from it
gives a closer look

                              if you look about
                          a star is shining and
                          there is passion and
                            peace for the heart

The narthex of St. Bartholomew's Church
is lined with made-ready cots like an
ancient mosaic; place to put down the
heads together, a home to conquer the night,
to strengthen, restore, to stretch full length,
free form the toes, pull up the legs,
slowly fold arms, hands to the heart, close
the eyes, sleep

in the innocence of the womb
under the shadows of Park Avenue.

Crosstown

from the 35th floor of my hotel room
looking down on Big River Hudson
and Broadway I was on the qui vivre.
Theatre! Dropped down in elevator's
bubble of lights to ground; crossed
over to Shubert Alley, paused at the
doorman's smile. Hold it ESTHER:

> thirty years ago, standing in line
> at high noon, 50 of us sliding together
> waiting to get in, be seen for open call,
> casting Equity, smash British play
> Rosencrantz and Guildenstern Are Dead, for Broadway
> production. An hour's wait! Finally
> inside theatre, walked across stage,
> handed stage manager pic and resume.
> <u>Thank you...next...</u>
> phone: 2 a.m., London needs another
> resume, yes, you are confirmed for audition,
> Alvin Theatre in two weeks. Be ready in
> scene from Shakespeare. We shall expect
> you? <u>Oh yes, yes, and thank you.</u> <u>Thank you</u>.

This Thanksgiving night clutching ticket ready
for eight o'clock curtain instead of 7:30 backstage
call (and you better be there or understudy alerted),
I moved with the crowd, but intent on my own musings;

> Audition. On time. I had spent every waking
> hour in study with a Shakespearian coach.
> Spent a week in Marblehead with my family

letting the sea wash me clean in learning
my lines! Return and ready. Wore my silver
heart and a light blue sheath dress. And
walked on stage under the hanging light bulb.
Still can feel that huge dark rise of silence.
Sensed bodies and I knew that they were <u>all</u>
out there...and with everything I had began:

Hamlet: Act IV, Scene VII

Queen: One woe doth tread upon another's heel
So fast they follow: - Your sister's drown'd, Laertes.

Laertes: Drown'd! O where?

Queen: There is a willow grows aslant a brook,
That shows his hoar leaves in the glassy stream;
There with fantastic garlands did she come
Of crow-flowers, nettles, daisies, long purples,
That liberal shepherds give a grosser name,
But our cold maids do dead men's fingers call them.
There on the pendent boughs her coronet weeds
Clambering to hang, an envious sliver broke,
When down her weedy trophies and herself
Fell in the weeping brook. Her clothes spread wide,
And, mermaid-like, awhile they bore her up,
Which time she chanted snatches of old tunes,
As one incapable of her own distress,
Or like a creature native and indued
Unto that element; but long it could not be
Till that her garments, heavy with their drink,
Pull'd the poor wretch from her melodious lay
To muddy death,

Laertes: Alas, then, is she drown'd?

> Queen: Drown'd, drown'd.

Professional theatre. Magnificent. Bringing to hold
to the white light within to all I know of it!
I thought back:

> awakened, late night in fever to hear:
> Miss Buffler, your schedule is...oh, yes
> you've been cast. This is your stage manager,
> and first rehearsals in N.Y., costume fitting,
> movement classes, then by bus to Washington D.C.,
> opening, two weeks, ready, return for B'way opening.
> Congratulations!

This was IT!!

Thirty years later, I can still hear the lyrical heartbeat.
Disciplines, I still know and use. It was a two-year run,
I never missed a performance.

Theatre, the very word still gives me life.

Museum Fever

GUGGENHEIM
METROPOLITAN
MOMA

                                        Matisse:
                                        PEOPLE
                                      hundreds
                                edging together
                                  eager to see
                                     feel paint
                                 all of it slash
                       against and into you
                               just this once

Opening Night Broadway

It was over.
Audience on their feet
gave us seven curtain calls!

Voiced out, exhilarated
wet in sweat,
the leading man (brilliant work)
coming off stage
bumped into the Producer.

I had come from crossover understage,
met them on stairs, heard the lead as
he asked money-bag man <u>how was it</u> ... <u>was it?</u>

Shrugged cynical reply,
<u>All actors are the same!</u>

I should have spit! SOB.

Seduction

*W*as in the haunting call of India.
Entering the chemist's shop of Caswell-Massey.
39th & Lex (always for me in NYC), and
approaching from the depths of many sparkling
glass displays was a middle-aged woman.
Her swirling skirt, mysterious in design;
eyes of seductive liquid mauve in color,
mouth of asking smiles, looked longingly at me.
Trembling, I was lost.
Galvanized to action, asked for a flask
of the costly, subtly irresistible fragrance,
Heliotrope.

> In a New England winter, cold of bone,
> I dab a drop of it behind my ear.
> A flower appears
> And I hear the blue of her voice.

In A Heap On The Floor Of A Bloomingdale's Elevator

how come? Needed shoes, 4th floor;
entering street floor level, I was attacked
by slick fashion models waving atomizers
and squirting obnoxious perfumes over me!
Escaping, I made a dash for the back
self-operated elevators.

Seven of us entered, three men, four women;
a slow rise; suddenly, the giant lift quit!
We were between floors. Men in command,
pushed the emergency button. Nothing. Again
they pushed, pushed. Nothing. Silence. Anxious.
Panic. Men began pounding the huge sealed doors.
Air fouled. More pounding, kicking, shouting. Ten
minutes imprisoned, my heartbeat heightened.
A lady held my hand, <u>are you alright?</u>
<u>Maybe</u>, I whispered. Her large round brown
Israeli eyes understood. She slipped off my coat,
folded it into a pad to the floor, sat me down,
took my hand. One woman worried about lunch,
the other, grim, stared, said nothing. The men
shouted furiously. Outside, voices, <u>coming</u>...
Engineers with crowbars slowly... pried open
the large solid steel door. We managed a smile,
and were taken aloft and out!

<u>Alright?</u>
<u>Yes.</u>
<u>Alright?</u>
<u>Yes.</u> <u>I'm so grateful.</u>

Holding hands tight, our eyes flicked,
smiled in sudden joy.
I walked to the escalator, waved,
saluted, waved g'bye...
lost in the melee of NYC.

Friends,
These Among Others

*J*oan lives in Brooklyn and you take the F train.
Subway. Each of us with coats drawn tight in recoil.
Quiet, almost a mutter as we note others.

An observation. A waiting.

Carroll Street; off alone late. Up the stairs
to walk a block to the garden gate
of a gardened brownstone; one flight walk-up
to enter her pad — creative stuff — art decor, books!
A perfume to the spirit follows for a few days.
It is her laughter that pulls me to wherever she lives.
Born New Yorker. Irish. She will never leave.
She insists I sleep in her new brass bed (she always
wanted one).
She paints. She writes.
On the town, she orders a Manhattan, straight-up.
Thanks.

*a*nd then there is Mary

Eastside Manhattan

Tiny condo looking to East River and UN.
We've known one another a space of years.
We're writers; our talk, bits of now, nostalgia.
There is unspoken harmony. Texas brought us together.

She a born one and still holds to that soft soothing speech.
I'm Eastern, was a former transplant, now back to N'east.
Her gathered antiques speak pride.
Late afternoon she invites me to the Plaza,
Palm Court for tea. Spiffy-dressed
we take the 1st Avenue bus to 57th, transfer
crosstown (what no cab?) Careful we've been.
But we feel the River, people, the streets.
It is still daylight. She's been mugged
going to church, eight a.m.; also had a foot run over
by a slow-braked truck. Bad stuff.
She never thought of leaving the city, living anywhere else...
locked within there is no other wash of life for her.
Early evening, our bus stops at 'Lex' and last person to get on
is an old woman. Black coat, bent, no hat, flying white hair.
<u>Wrong bus lady.</u> Calm, patient driver gets her carefully off the
bus, giving directions for
the right bus.

                                        This is NEW YORK!?

We get off at Fifth, tally-ho around Bergdorf's
to the Plaza, stand in line to the Palm Court.
Seated with grace to an elegant Victorian doeskin sofa
under crystal chandeliers.
Seasoned cummerbunded waiters flashed smiles and charm.
Sighs from violin, piano, cello fluttered over us
as we devoured Devonshire cream and scones.
We chatted in mood about things, people we knew and loved.

                                        Maybe our last time...

I was leaving in the morning.

Going out under the canopy I felt
the golden thread of theatre unraveling
over me...hearing the sweet sound of song

♪...On A Clear Day... and
I'm above on the 2nd floor bay
looking to the fountain having
cocktails, seated next to the stars
(Yves and Barbra). Director
Mr. Minelli having placed me there
(an extra) and hearing him
in quiet, firm voice say
<u>Mr. Montand, Miss Streisand</u>
(her skin magnificent) <u>this film
is in English. We will take it again.</u>
We did. It was a "wrap"!

Did my face end up on the cutting room floor?
No. 30 years ago, noontime, dark glasses, scarf tied low
around face, head, I slinked into a Yorktown movie-house
where the film was having its first NY run...
waiting...waiting...suddenly, a face large as life
flicked on. MINE. At the Plaza.

<u>CAB!</u> Central Park deepened dark.

Penn Station

Amtrak

Trains posted: Boston 11:10 on time.
Struggling down narrow stairs to the 'bowels',
baggage heaving, shoulder strap constantly
slipping, breath heavy in the tired air
of lower train shed...and there she comes!
Slithering in like a plump dark grey electric eel,
mouth sliding open waiting (maybe 3 mins.)
to gobble up its victims!

<u>Spatio temporal.</u>

Get in girl, we're rolling, going north,
Boston, going home.

Still Life 1990

Sorting out few turnip chips
under duck legs humility rises
as
the view across the East River
from the River Cafe
under spinning cables
of the Brooklyn Bridge
jellies the mind:
Manhattan.

Much time, the chef presents
<u>le déjeuner chef-d' oeuvre</u>
two ample duck legs,
six very green peaked haricot vert,
tiny scarce carrot strips,
one long watercress;
this settled in a vrai salt
brown sauce floating five white beans
and three turnip chips. Hard rolls.
Touchable exquisite fresh flowers.
Silence.

The Old Gal peeks from far harbor.
Stick the thumb firmly into
the soul-hole of the palette.

Reawakened November One, 1991

*t*o feel the deep cut;
the scar on which forever
will hang his face
upon my heart;
the ache for his presence;
always <u>theatre.</u>

This morning. Shakespeare's folio
opened and ghosts slid forth,
hand in hand, chanting and dancing
a welcome and carried him aloft;
Joseph Papp! Hamlet spoke;
<u>My pulse, as yours, doth temperately
keep time ...</u>

Vienna

> I love you Ludwig
> need to feel you close
> need to brush your arm
>
>

7 a.m. on my window sill
baroquely fluffed, ready on wing
the pigeon was magnificent,
calling me to Heligenstadt,
the street of one of Ludwig's
countless homes.

It was wooded countryside then
but it must have been the linden
tree's lure that touched his ears.
It stood in a closed courtyard
circled by warm-colored worn stones.
Did he hesitate, climbing the wooden
stairs leading onto the narrow balcony,
pausing, before entering the bare
square workroom where in a corner
his piano waited? Ripping forth
agonies of oncoming deafness which
only he understood... "oh, you people,
who consider me... a misanthrope ...
you know not the true cause..."

It was middle day, laden with storm.
Tourists heated up the dismal workroom.
Our breaths dimmed the glass-covered cases.

Eyes peered at faded scores, personal
letters, photographs; tired plants drooped
under small windows.

Shortly, the caretaker released a cassette.
It blared forth snatches, patches of his
Fifth! Shattered, I fled the room,
stood trembling, reaching to the linden.

Sharp wind. December gale. In suddenness,
a ball of sun burst open the snow clouds.
The old tree calmed, and he stood with me.

7s

*W*hat I know enough, as much
I dare to speak.

It is to bud a song
to the very, very green of the maple,
the cheery red of the cheerful cherry,
the laughing tassel of the swingin' birch,
the languishing stalk of hawthorn's hope,
wine to the mind

to again glide up the Danube to Melk,
stand on the parapet of the Benedictine
monastery; "fortified house" (1049), given
to kindle love. Take hand in hand across
the balcony and enter the library. Grey,
damp to the body but gold to the soul it is
to look upon nine thousand books written
in Latin and printed in gold; manuscripts,
documents, and incunabula!

to then munch a warm pretzel
from the village coffee house, the bus ride
back to Vienna, a pleasurable bounce.

This day it is May in New England.
Opening buds. Ecstasy is.

— *for Jean Pedrick*

The Pummerin* Bell

Like fresh water, hurtling
harmonics through a dark night,
Christmas Eve, St. Stephen's Cathedral,
Vienna, 1990.

The bell calls, distant, now closer;
our eyes upward, breaths cold, misty,
as thousands enter, nudge for space
among the cathedral's towers. The bell
booms, booms out clutching the heart,
the mind. The organ in crescendo startles,
then quiets to young boys' voices lifting
eerily from the choir loft, singing
the Mass. Gowned trumpeters magically
appear on a side balcony, triumphant
in golden sound! The procession begins,
moves forward in floating rhythms of light
toward the altar.

The bones of this old Protestant sit upon
a hard bench facing a small center altar.
Above the communion table is a painting
of a woman, ordinary dress, darkish curly
hair, celestial eyes. She leans, presents
to the world a healthy baby, naked.
Overtones from the bell's ringing...
<u>Where do I stand with all this?</u>
<u>Could I become a Catholic?</u>
Religions burn through me.
Ruminate upon all those people gathered in Vienna
over the centuries. The Celts, Slavs,
French, Hungarians, Turks, Richard the Lion-Hearted,

Jews, Nazis, Austrians... Mozart's funeral...
I sit in tired humility...
my Eucharist, a continuum-communion.

Gradually, all becomes creased up like a child's
folded paper airplane swirling among towers,
seeking release. The great bell tolls exuberantly
as it leads, however for each, through heavy,
worn flapping protective entry curtains,
out into the oncoming gray of another Christmas morning.

In this New World, at odd moments,
the sound of the bell closes in over me.
Passionately, the strength of its sound holds,
calms, gives time to know more of myself.
Truth; this moment and whatever is ahead
for another day.

Nickname, boomer; forged from Turkish war cannon (1683); the 45 thousand lb. bell was struck with hammers, i.e., "boomer". Later, 1945, Battle for Vienna, as the Cathedral was burning, it crashed to the ground. Fragments reforged; Provinces contributed. It is 9 feet high, 13 feet around; rings 3 times a year: Christmas Eve, New Year's Day, Easter.

New Orleans

Never get over it,
roll it on the tongue,
turns me like the riverboat's

paddle wheel . . . MIS--SIS--SI--PPI . . . ♪♪

great arms swingin' out
touching life. Steamy mouth
open wide, singin' the blues
on its way to the sea.

Mother's Breakfast

*G*o!
The bell sounds!
Five gallon kettle of grits
fresh made from the kitchen
brought out front to serve
hungry, happy people.
Savor the bits-baked ham,
biscuits, red beans and rice
with sausage, eggs, chicory coffee,
and bread pudding!

I'll meet you there. Soon!

Beaux Arts

Merleen, Merleen ♪
of New Orleans . . . ♪

Songbird.
Face like a Creole queen.
Graceful, tall, old, lean,
she swipes away others'
crumbs, juices, leftovers.
In starched shirtwaist,
she smiles down
at her cleaned tables.

She works at MOTHER's.
A third generation menial

<u>Merleen. Like my name?
My own mother's
WHITE LADY said to call
the baby after her. Me</u>

Merleen . . . ♪

I have her picture.
I wish her to come
with me!

<u>To God, I wish I could.
Never been wher'else</u>

New Orleans . . . ♪

A Burning Thorn

It came together at MOTHER's
food
headed into us
with talk.
The stature of him
all together small, neat,
in peaked blue cap, thread-
washed jacket and jeans,
round, peering into glasses

Me: What adds it up?
        What do you do?

Him: Run a home for homeless.

Me: O, I guess you are
        bogged down with a lot
        of hangers-on?

Him: You're wrong. They
        all work. Discover
        the thing in them
        within. We feed, bed,
        hope on . . . .
        What about you?

Me: Maybe same kind of thing.
        Get it down whenever
        it rears its risen head.

Smiles. Soda biscuits, coffee,
beans and gravy for us!

Old Cemetery New Orleans

Encrusted high iron gate. Easing through,
I felt suspended tramping down the paths,
reading on memorial slabs of stone
the names of men and women buried beneath the even
so quietly sinking graves.
Smell of a musty burning? Was it a faraway
drumming, the spirits of voodoo that brought
me here as I moved among the dead — my footsteps
making soft over leaves, ground spices,
grated bones mixed with pungent fish oils?
Or was it the smell of sauces from a Creole kitchen
wafting through the city? Finding the name of a first
French settler, was it the toe of his worn boot poking forth
as a gnarled knot of bush? Or a Spanish grandee's eye
oozing up in lust, struggling for life? Still under trance,
hypnotized,
would I witness the proud British duke lying in blood
from musket fire from one of "Old Hickory's" frontiersman?
Was that the haunting whine of a saxophone
coming from a delta bar? Blacks in sweat from stench
of a slave ship just arrived from Africa waiting in harbor?
Was old Voodoo Queen Marie Laveau fixin' me?
I paled trembled for an exegesis.

Mists of evening twisted in from the Gulf.
A shroud descended over the tombs — I fled.

The Garden District

*N*o bus allowed. Walk.
Quiet feet to her home.

Flounced lady awaits
on the steps of her house;
bright smile, brightened
copper colored hair, long
curled so; she floats, legs
being caressed under chiffon
orangey gown. Softly spoken words of welcome.

The women on the tour are seduced.
She leads us through rooms of
period antiques: silver lustre,
flip glass, cream figurines, delft,
toiles de Jouy, Chippendales, rugs,
exquisite rarities, paintings..
step softly dear hearts.
She is witty. She sets limits,
'not to go upstairs', 'Not to linger.'
The half-hour is fading. Sweeping on,
a large dark room looms. Very mahogany.
There, reaching to the ceiling, stands
a huge bookcase! Its narrow wood-crossed
glass paneled doors give forth a murky,
mysterious enchantment. She points...
<u>William Pitt's bookcase...</u>

<u>Which one.</u> <u>Daddy or son?</u>
Did she hear me?
Sudden translucent waft of white

light enveloped her - exquisite
burning odor ... was this solely
my own poetic creation?
She fluttered in front of the tour
ladies with a telling, cheerful and
smiling wave of good-byes?

Lovely lady, some summer night
when the Big River Moon calls to the
Spirits to dance in your house, you
may find me there. Unannounced.
Footfall under the live oaks.

<u>Pssst...William,</u>
<u>hold my hand,</u>
<u>you've the key?</u>

Berkeley

                    It all comes back
                    like the woman in
                    panama hat banded
                    with decadent black lace

                    or when I stood before
                    a psycho colored mike
                    at Subterranean Vals
                    and read my lilac poem
                    and shook

                    or when dressed to the nines
                    Patricia looked me over,
                    <u>no</u> <u>fur,</u> <u>Ess</u>

                    or sweet soul it was
                    with the camellias

but mostly camellias
what a way to be
as wild Pacific washes
into the spirit,
enters the cells,
strips you clean
to begin again.
It is to dream,
rise to life.

I am the land, to roll, fall
at any moment with deep kneel

to the sea. Climb, climb
the hills. Day and all night
be with the camellias,
reminders of what we are,
what we have to give.

Chicle Tree
Guatemala

The chicle tree
still hovers over me.
tall
gives a strange cry
in the rain forest's
ruins
Tikal.

King "Ah Kakau"
(Lord Chocolate)
sips his dark drink
pleads to the Gods
from the sacrificial
pyramids
inscribes a glyph-
bundle of 20 sticks
record of time.

Now slithery grass
comforts his bones
and the chicle tree
weeps sweet juice-
dripping tears upon mounds
of Mayan dead.
Its gum sticks
to the roof of my mouth.

Dialogue

Fumes of petroleum hit the face
from the gold plated water faucet
in the elegant condo bathroom.

Drive slowly down Fannin.
Wonder at the block after block
of fresh flowers waiting on shelves,
no one buying, holding them.
Where do they end?

Hi Missus! the black Stetson hatted
cowboy enters HO-JOs carrying a bulging
black plastic trash bag. What's ya duffel?
Worn jeans hug his warked skinny legs.
RODEO! Good show! 63 thou' - patient,
cat-eyed drivers like night creepers
crawling home under a Texas wet moon.

Waiting at the Supermart's parking lot,
suggestion: flip the locks on your
car doors.

Mattie: the compound's security guard;
the quality of her eyes; our black and white
fingers twined together in greeting;
her low, low voice and open smile;
hungry hearts; nothing hazy between us.

Unshy canyons of phallic sculptures of steel.
Father of Medicine Hippocrates as sculptor.

Carving out lives.

Plotted greens for the Academes savoring
the edging forward young and spirited.

In city, the Arts strike forth from every corner.
Name them. Inescapable. They're yours.
Stoplights for the nerves.

<u>What</u> is it that burns in the heart of this city?
Exhibits itself?
Soundings from the Gulf forced upward, inland,
bringing a chimerical light to all it reaches, touches?
Kicks the soul. Builds and at times
overwhelms the body.

A new culture from the edge of the World - Houston

Part Three
New England

Portsmouth Sunday On The Coast, New Hampshire

Sacre printemps.
The sun births easily
out from the womb
of the North Atlantic.

It gives passionate cry
to the Earth. Stretches in warmth
to the waiting buds next door.
Ready they are - the maple, birch,
cherry, and the hawthorn.

Nature brings us the wine.
Holy red.

Hurricane Rose

Two gulls in a shrieking delirium
lashed at my bay. White winged in
horror they headed inland to the
Piscataqua's North Pond. They knew.
I felt it! The blow was if Orpheus,
flagellant in waves mounting from the
North Atlantic beating upon his lyre
and in song calling in wild longing
for Eurydice. But looking back it
could be death. The sky already a
deathlike dark covering shroud. A
terrible tempest. I flattened down.
Within time, the hurricane wind
whined itself into billowing folds
and tiptoed into the bowels of Mt.
Agamenticus.
To feel the calm. A rejuvenescence.

Looking upon a new world. Splotches
of vermilion and glorious bronze
looked upward from the maples.
I struggled to stand and turned
to stare at the red rose on my work
table. A loving kindness gift from
poets.

Tensed wires of minds we had been.
Working under uncertainty, courage,
hope, agony and stress, always
believing, unforced and alive, but
with inside selves at risk.

Beat upon your lyres.
Songs to cry out
and to be heard.

O Dear God

Out of the hide-out-hole of winter!
Sun enters: toes unmesh, bodies
seen, feet center stage begin a strong
march onto the earth; people look up
and lift their faces to smile.

From my Fifth floor window
a shawl of buds spreads, pulls me down
grasping flaying into the trees birch
hawthorn maple and cherry soothing
my face hearing siren winds hard rains
nude to southern sun wheresoe'er passion
felt in breath knowing a season's life
the wry candor of a cell's death.

O Dear God it is May June
in New Hampshire

and I stand in the bush calmed, be-
wildered as the balm closes over
the days in fragrance of lilacs!
Soon the heat of summer will settle
and the ambrosia fade.

I will bring lilacs to you,
bury your head deep into them
for my love awaits you there.

Seasons

The cactus hangs by the window
near my bed; opens its heart
to bloom, dropping blood,
white and red as one
at Christmas, 1991/
to be eighty

and remember

Wildflowers

grow in a box on my rooftop.
This is a very small space;
a framed New England summer
portrait. Bumblebees buzz
<u>a fortiori</u>. A color mix.
A wind melody, weird and wild
in dance and sun. Alone in hum
to the moon I am. The sea rolls,
boils to a blow, and the wildflowers
flatten, then straighten,
shake, drop ready seedcakes!

Prescription

The on-going patient
staggered forth
to her rooftop flower box.

Flowers in bloom in a small space.

> Space. Caught off balance.
> In a much washed cotton robe.
> Cold, cold x-ray slab.

But this moment a woman alone.
No strain. It is to kiss
each flower-face: poppies, cosmos,
nicotiana, bee balm in bees, curry,
absinthe, ginger mint, lanterns,
Susan plant, blue grass, lavender,
borage, lettuce, Johnny-jump-up,
clover, long purples, dill;
all eased dyes for the veins.

A confidence; quick set threads
of Nature. Use aplenty.

> From one soft friable soil to another;
> balloon flower, Platycodon mariesii 'blue',
> blooming time summer through frost . . .
> perennial. Esther.

Ace
and the whirrrr of his bicycle

And there he was! Long white hair
tied back in neat pigtail (old hippie)
always a comeuppance.
Once, only once, on an early April
morning on the Square I heard the whirrrr stop.
He handed me a small, stalky bunch
of pussywillows. His soft grey kitteny eyes
smiled. He said
<u>It's April</u>

Now he's dead.

Each April, into the round hole of my favorite
blue flower bowl I arrange tender soft buds.
Sit quiet. Very quiet caressing them.
If feels like an old woman stroking,
pushing away her winter's skin.

Day Lilies

The New England farmer stopped mowing,
smiled at me and handed over the fence
a bunch of day lilies ('over the hill' laughter).

    Inside me again, a ten year old
    flouncing about youngster thinking to pretty-up
    our old farm house parlor, I had picked
    armloads of day lilies. Some from behind
    the barn's outhouse; around the boarded-up old
    well grew aplenty; a few kept pace with the
    pink and cream hollyhocks leaning against
    the house and outside cellar door.
    A breeze said 'hello' from the paperboy's
    newspapers thrown over the fence! The sound
    of walnuts plunging down off the old tree
    hitting the tin roof of the pigpen; my tired
    sunburned arms giving the hand-pump
    an extra squeaky pull, lifting a drink of deep well water.
    Be sure to hang the tin cup back on the grape arbor!
    At dusk, in wonder watching the huge flapping
    wings of a night bird hovering and dipping low
    over Ridge Valley creek.

The farmer's wrinkled face breathed
near mine, grained like a golden field
of laid down freshly cut summer wheat.
My cheeks flushed in stamina of day lilies.

Jolted

Coming upon the satiny old mare standing
in sleep on our Village Square, hitched
to an open carriage. Her driver smiled
wide in waiting for tourists.
Again they come to Portsmouth town.
Warm their veins on 'back then': potato-
growing Abenakis among banks of strawberries;
the Crown; the Colonies; traders and fisher-
folk of the Piscataqua. . .

Sharp pull to the bridle, slap of reins,
the old horse 'came to', and moved. . .
'giddap ol' girl !'

The message hit me hard. Age.
My need for the raw, primal earth, all life.
No panic but a wildness began. Go:

With a sing a ding a ding a ding
ride, bike, walk three miles west
of town to Village Newington.
Like an east wind fetch of waves
on the Great Bay, the heart leaps!
Small tufts of fog rise and the
smell of salt marsh closes in.
There is knocking at the heart
as we go through the gate entering
together all creatures free:
Great Bay National Wildlife Refuge.

Slow down...go back, go back,
think ice. Million years of mile
deep slabs of it... began to quiver
in melt. The mud and crud crept in
and life from the sea; fish, birds
winged through tempests onto new land,
creatures of kinds, man.
Pawtucket Indians quiet in peace, happy
for what nature gave. Musket fire! Drums!
Bold pioneers took over, worked the land,
gave voice to new ways. Lived well; farmed,
raised cattle, finest apples. Life
in seasons, tough among cheerful hard-
working, god-fearing neighbors.
Early nineteen fifties rumors came
then more... then the fact! 4,000 acres
for an Air Force Base next door. Name, Pease.

New sounds; controversy; bomber's drone.
History threaded Newington earth jittered.
Loyal loving heritage folk hung true
to church, parsonage and old town hall
as bones in their beautiful cemetery shook.

Time nipped into time. Forty years later,
summer 1991, it was sunset for Pease AFB!
Like the old horse ready to move forward
peace in the world, the Feds and Congress
slapped its reins giving the westernmost
parcel of the Base to U.S. Dept. Fish and
Wildlife. Newington rose to the challenge,
gift of itself, land of the Bay in praise
together preserve us free!
Great Bay National Wildlife Refuge:

Ghosts of ready bombers side by side
on the grassy island

give way, pleased, amused,
to the long legged upland sandpiper
scratchin' out a nest. New home...
hurry, not many of you left.

Through the gate. Elongate,
wild as a child wild in the wild,
openmouthed
watch the rare yellow-breasted chat
flip a tail sitting upon an unused
solemn bomb storage bunker.

Move in the quiet. Look into the blue.
Astounded, sitting on an abandoned
telegraph pole, the fish-eating osprey
has found a new home! The shivery
bizarre 'concertina' protective wire
fence spins free in welcome. Its
glittery metal eyes gleam.

Take the early cart tracks as footpaths
rambling through the oak and pine scrub
to top of the knoll to find turn of time
Margeson house. Now the restored Refuge
Center. Art as portrait to the Great Bay!
The soul melts to the handling choice water-
washed seductive stones gathered and used
as support for the porte-co.chere and
side porch. Inside; books, photographs,
slide shows, special lectures...
roll with wisdom hidden in Nature.

Below, heading toward the Bay, showy sumac
borders open field. Enchantment under a Fall
sunflecked sky. Hand to a beating heart, to see
stepping from a tall bank of wild purple asters
a family of deer... buck, doe and fawn...

wondrous eyes ask love. No fear.
No hurry... as the afternoon breaks in beauty.

A light wind skips in from Agamenticus
The field narrows toward a narrow point
reaching into the Bay. Is that a gundalow
waiting, strong men to row? Or the old
ferries' stop? Birds call. Ancient
red and white pines shadow, cover the way,
their seed bundles wing down as soft carpet.
Sun tips the rangy bare top branched aged
white pine. Rest stop and watch tower for the
now so few bald eagles! Luck holds. Here
it comes . . . white head and tail and gorgeous
dark body plummets down over the Bay, then
rises, feathers like a violin's pizzicato,
lands in grace on top branch of the pine.
Breathless, man and bird.

Ducking branches along the rim of the Bay,
alerted to a long ahoooooooo again ahuuoooooo
and streaking out of the woods two thin coyotes!
Nervous chipmunk, tail up, trying to escape.
How did coyotes find this salt marsh? Will
they stay or are they off trail to the west?
Tucking away notebook and field binocs , air
was startled by a covey of wild turkeys in flight!

Mystery unfolds in the wilderness . . . ahead,
some one thousand acres where no person is
allowed to tread, all creatures in the wild
alone in their own ways.
Look closely in wonderment, what is that wrinkled
dark head rising out of the Ponds? Monster? Turtle?
a 200 lb.-er diggin' around in the scud for supper;
its babies at risk, tough life for turtles.

Dusk and a chill creeps in. Button up. Fall, and
soon winter . . . Overhead a whirl of Canadian
geese heading south tunes in with a soft clacking
of dropping hazelnuts. A huge gray squirrel
twitches a tail. Group of black ducks bob-talk
in an evening's gossip. Cormorants like waiting
theatre-goers standing in line for the big show
of oysters! Mourning doves and whippoorwills and
loons seduce in tantalizing tender song.
Is that the red-headed or the red-bellied woodpecker
knocking at the door of a red pine telling all,
'here for the winter'! Noisy black backed gulls
insist a call 'come back'. The old barred owl
is awake, sits high in an oak, winks, neats its
feathers, eyes down at a skittery field mouse,
gives a night call and takes off.

Like the delight of fresh fruit at night,
the smell of tide gives lift, ahummm to taste
for fish; smelt, eel, striped bass, alewife.
Birds of color mix; falcon, blue heron, scaup,
dowitcher; darkened clouds of v-leader geese
flying south to happy hunting grounds; lone
hawk rises high, swoops low to the Bay, screams.

Weaving along the Bay's rim, tired legs. mud
on boots, take a last stand on a final lookout,
wooden platform. On the railing is a celestial-
winged dragonfly. It has had its fill of mosquitos
this day and has landed here to die. A drop of
moisture shimmers on the magnificent netted
iridescent wings. A touch to the long slender
body and the drop disappears. Move toward the gate.
Peace overtakes. Streaks of red like on a loved worn
quilt tuck in the sky.

Aeolus, god of the winds whispers in, then cries out, knocks caps high in salute! Quiets, twirls the wind-harp to a new song. AGE. Hold hands, feel the small rustle of being.

Refuge; lead us here again, bring us to the Song.

The Cricket Call

Is this the winter, a cold one,
only middle of September,
but there she is!
Rooftop, five flights up, farm
flower box fulsome in bloom, shines
in the sea's wind under a red moon.
Her call startles. Warning?
". . . hang to, hang on . . ." insists
itself like an unexpected crackle
of a shoulder bone softly breaking
the night like a wayward highwayman
chanting a love song in secret under
broad leaved red nasturtiums . . .

December. The wood is stacked.
The 'downs' reach out comfort.
Kitchen herbs dried, ready and
fragrant for pot of soup. Window
panes glaze. Sky darkens. Snow.
The bedroom's white cactus twists
its green jagged stems toward the sun,
ends pushing out into pure starlike blooms
tinged in red. Rushing a little
the soul unfolds.
Call, call little cricket . . .   . . .

Breaking The Tomb Of Winter

Returning home
feathering into the loving kindness
of the familiar pillow,
there in a cosseted corner
I found my prize avocado
waiting to be carried away
in death!
I caressed its chalky leaves
now withered like aged skin.
I crumbled them as they fell
to the floor. All except one.

Thoughts crept back from the visit.
The rivers of living waters
were not mine. One week. Ready
to return. Then I felt the grace
of the lake's bald eagle
riding on its high-low thermals.
Roll with the new; wordplays;
high-tech, put the 'mouse' in place;
fresh tastes in hyped cuisine, veggies,
beans; walk the extra mile to listen;
observe family. Fax love, trees, rain,
flowers, sunset, witching southern moon,
grandchildren; good heartbeat running
by the river; nothing sour.
There was no dark side.

Figure the avocado.
Quiet and alone in a room. Cold. Waiting.
Looking south from the still closed window,
its bare straight green stem shows a notched
new leaf edging skyward.

--for Monique and her loving assistance

Newmarket Public Library
New Hampshire

1884, red brick, high on a knoll,
hot in the sun looking down
to the Lamprey river.
A solo in song of autumn gold,
the first-grader jumps high into the leaves!
He holds close to his chest a book.
His first take-home library book.
He stood on tiptoe checking it out.

Faraway, Old Man of the Mountain
flips open his record book, settles down,
and scores another notch to the granite.

Forest Hill Farm
New Hampshire
December 1989

*B*lack skeletal maples stood
straight up; frostings of snow
lingered in winter-scored notches.
Below on the bank North Wind
slapped at the weather-beaten sugarhouse.
Thermometer read: <u>zero.</u>

Evergreens dusted off, the snow-drifted road
escaped uphill to the barn; two cats moused in;
chickens cooped with no-scratch forage
awaited Mr. Rooster's strut and call;
no eggs today!

The thirty sheep nudged together
in sun in the V of the corner fence;
creamy backs of heavy wool graced
by thin black and ivory legs, slicked
over in white like a huge cake.
Codfather the ram rustled his readiness.
Winter born lambs in pen chanted
soft baas as they nuddled along
the ewe's hard nipples.
Morning and evening. the lady shepherd
with watchful eye and strong arm
lugged the bale of hay from the barn,
lifted it high over the fence, bucketed
the grain, and watered the flock!

Lambs quieted in the manger.
Reds and golds streaked the cold
western sky... awaited the Star.

Larke, the soft-eyed sheep dog barked,
released in leaps of joy, pushed
against the chest, knocked at heart's
childhood remembered song:
come let us run, let us play in the snow,
come let us run, let us play in the snow,
down we go, down we go, down in the soft white snow...

Another chunk to belly of woodstove!
Smoke rose from the chimney in crystalline
strings like a prelude played in an enchanted land of
warmth, laughter and love:
Christmas.

—for Nancy

A Summer's Wreath
the linnet's song

A cooling wind off Mt. Monadnock brings in
a ballata. Perennials and annuals border
the granite walkway. Blow kisses!

The seventh month old wreath hangs flat
against the wall of the farmhouse porch.
Flusters its dried detritus in welcome.
Ah, those pioneering house finches!
They skim in, flutter up the wreath, peck,
clean out stems, carry in nips of wool
from ram Codson's back, work it all together
into a cup-shaped deep nest. Such goings on
... His rose red head and breast, her
quiet brown-streaked body and wings lift
my eyebeams! The <u>carpodacus mexicanus</u>
have arrived! Stay quiet and watch.

Naturally, soon three finely speckled bluish
eggs come to being in the house finches' house.
She settles in, incubates, and waits.
He behaves with hysteric chirp, bringing
her seeds, fruit, choice morsels. Two weeks
and scrawny heads bob, peer out from the nest
screeching <u>give us food</u>! They're ravenous,
eat everything brought in, sing, shake out
new wings, tumble forth from the nest, fly
in grace, ready for the woods and sky;
the finch family has flown their home.

Deep into summer. Busy days. Haymaking
and sheep to move from pasture to pasture.
Barbecue in the yard and supper on the porch!
<u>Let's get rid of that old wreath!</u>

A heavy blow and rain during the night had hit
the porch. Now stillness to the morning.
The wreath hanging at a wild angle, all at once
became lyrical! New, old songs came rollick-
ing forth and his raspberry head lifts, hits
the sun. In her beak, a bent twig with snips
of this and that, shadows on wing;
<u>they're at it again!</u>
The linnet's song is heard in the land.

Part Four
A Jugful Of Other Poems

Jugful

From the beginning
Age three. Pennsylvania
Schwenkfelder Sunday School.
Children's Christmas performance.
Then as now it was words, sound,
feelings, audience.
Lifted to the platform, given
the nod to recite the memorized
four line Jesus verse, I looked
upon the filled church and said:
<u>Here I stand on two little chips,</u>
<u>do come kiss my ruby little lips.</u>

Mother lifted me down and I sat
between grandfather (beard jiggling),
grandmother (velvet toque pushed in place
over wide brown eyes), mother and father
holding my hands.
It all felt right.

It is to dip into days
like thrusting arms into cool waterglass,
lifting with care the eggs to be carried
upstairs for the baking.
Join me for the warmth and smell of freshly
baked bread; be with my thoughts
as they rise...

A Beatitude

Teddy
the three-legged dog next door
whose run to be free
catches me
with the wind that pushes strong
over the Texas cedar brake.

Teddy, a 'hit-and-run'
one leg hanging, had been
found in blood; taken in love,
healed, given to live.

Tied mostly,
but when let free to run,
leaps, shakes saliva, pants, barks,
swings his tail with what he knows,
shares on 'those three'
in blessedness.

Gifts

Personal Ad

thinking
that one day perhaps
thinking one day you
may find me and I you
as my subconscious
continues to reach out
to the conscious and
in the meantime thinking
to lay my head next
your neck
Betty Goldstein

Le Tulipe Noire

Title of a novel
remembered only
for the struggle
in translation?

A dark tulip bulb
sits in old pewter,
waiting to bloom.
The gift, a reminder
not to be indifferent,
completely, to her
sustained crises
of fidgety collations.

Writer And A Fish

AHA! Shout out.
As a fisherman
by shores of Galilee?

It was Minneapolis
Minnesota. And
I looked upon a book
FISHING FOR BUFFALO.

Amazement, it was
about a strange fish!
Sucking fresh water
beauty, large in head
and body, fascinating.

Suddenly, I took the bait.
I was hooked, felt a deep,
dark water energy,
struggle, freedom,
desperation, mystery . . .
flipped to surface.
Reeled in.

--For grandson Robert

fly ash

hold in the hand a bottle
of grey fly ash garnered from
industrial fossil-burning
smokestacks

take the handful of a friend's ash
from the firkin let stream
and mountain caress his released
bones

watch the carnival of the
corps de ballet of lambs
as they rush the gentle slope
then stop

time now to remember the ash
leap through the pasture
hear my cry you
living and the dead

--for Charles

Lenny Tree
the Moharimet kind

He held it up, out to me,
a sopped wet paper napkin
wrapped around scraggly, dangling
roots of tiny green needle-balls
of a fir tree ...
A present!
We were poets
(six and seventy).
No one kidded us,
we knew, really,
what's in the hug of a poem.

Planted outside
with another pine
on my rooftop, it has made it
through two tough winters.
It's the real thing.
It's name (of course)
is Lenny.

> Among a lot of dirty letters
> foolscap, a great great
> grandfather had married
> Ann Donaghey ...
> written in, in pencil.

Visitation

In winter's ice cube
it was heartwarming to see
that a meltdown had begun
in the aqueousness of enough.
It had been a very long
looking out time ...

There they were. Two pigeons
alighting on the roof together
loving enough to be loved
as released from a snare.

A mounting rhythm felt.
Peculiar. As

> <u>Lifted from the Liffey,</u>
> <u>Floundered in Irish sea:</u>
> <u>hit the Scottish highlands,</u>
> <u>crying, longing to be home,</u>
> <u>Ann Donaghey</u> ...

And there in the room sat a duck!
Ordinary bird, plump, singing
with a merry heart; a gift
this day of a million hearts.

Daylight Saving

An uncommon experience
to float in absentia, unaware
when walking through the morning.
Could it be perhaps, like death,
unaware bit by bit of time
and place & change?
In the living arena, it was a startle
to the moving self pattern.
But a calming situation in asking
how much one really needs
to be ahead or behind in time?
Fuddle with the clock if you will.

In A Disfigured World

the young bat on my bathroom floor
coming into day there it lay,
blind, flapping its pouch asking
to be taken softly in hand
raise its head to fly, to live.

Somalia, summer 1992
millions of eyes awake asking
for food, not dried grass, not camel hide,
see again large-eyed lolling heads,
mouths open flapping ... drooling ...
hunger ... hunger ... water ... to live;
mother holds her child in shrunken
belly pouch, lies prone,
dies
as tribal pickup truck careens in;
gathers up skin bodies, bodies,
bones.

A Cadence

You mentioned, <u>Alhambra</u>,
it all came back
textless
but in sound:
France, Venice, Florence,
Rome, Switzerland, Como, Spain,
and then again Paris,
Concarneau, Quimperle, then
Granada and straight to the bed,

now alone it was to be.
The gate opened wide...
wide...you disappeared...

Robert
my breath rises with dew
walking the hill, the gate
to the Alhambra,
searching for the secret
that was you, me to join.

Patio de los Leones!
I peer from a dangerously
high outcrop of stone dropping
to a secret ledge in far hills
while the wild rose
scratches at my nose,

and the young stonecutter
eye for me asking for cigarettes
and suggesting his gift which
remains of what it could have been
still remains.

Elizabeth Alexandria Booth Wold

Like an August summer's bough

>wild, wild cherry tree
>hanging heavy in blood juice
>waiting in Maine's coastal wind
>to be cut loose in birthing fruit,

She comes.

Sweet Death Houses

In a cumulus cloud of white hair,
pristine, in elegant pink gown,
round, starflower eyes, she was
cornered in a wheelchair; a
shimmering watercolor. A portrait.
Unable to hug (damned chair),
a nurse swept in ... her professional
hand placed a tray of soft foods
in front of the 'portrait'.
I remembered how close we were;
her silver tea service, bone china,
linen napkins, and books of poetry
to read. Now my friend's lips moved,
no speech, just munched mashed
potatoes, vigorously. I was never
once recognized. I cried. A shake
of the nurse's head. Nothing said.

There she is, holed up
with a small group, sitting
in a wheelchair, in a dark
room, smoking. A beautiful
woman, so knowing, sophisticated,
bright, travelled, imperious.
She welcomes me and we grab hands,
as we push on to her double room.
Why in God's name is she here?
I know, have heard the logic
of the move, but we don't speak
of that. We laugh, gossip ...
until a sudden mood change.
She demands, <u>where is my lunch,
it's late!</u>

I visited him, slipped my hand
into his and together gave
each other the salute! <u>Carry on
smartly!</u> He sat as if in parade
dress hearing the army's bugle call
retreat! His t.v. droned on...
turned it off.
I remembered his step at my front
door, the carefully rolled offering
as tribute, the ARTS & LEISURE
section of the Sunday New York Times.
A longing lay close.

I kissed his thin-skinned cheek.
At the door, turned to wave
goodbye. He had nodded off,
head dropped, eyes closed.

A gentleman of soft voice and calm mien.
I bend close. You don't know me? Esther.
Remember, summer theatre matinee.
The luncheon in Connecticut. A delight.
Taking your arm after church; picking up
your paper and then breakfast. And again
your arm in mine to safely cross the
street? Our talks on the town's history.

He is blind. My heartbeat skips
thinking on that day he appeared
unannounced with a large bunch of home-
grown garden flowers, carefully tendered
in a rusting tin can.

Kick wide the pretty painted doors,
all you people 'resting' in waiting-
out-death-houses. Glide out swiftly,
hobble if necessary, leave the stifling
boxes, fly forth the wheelchairs
like gathering birds of paradise...

Last Rites
He Has It

There he sat
sprawled in a chair
family numb beside him
at a raucous cocktail party.

He was so pale.
Galvanized
we stood listening to

Accolades. Cumbersome word
to match a pyramid of thought
gathered to an understanding,
a loving, a hate in despair
to his last being there.

Where does the mind land
sitting in on your own funeral service?
Was this his wish for a good laugh, shout
to life among friends; a defiance; fierce
reckoning; acceptance; an ego jaunt?
Whatever. Good show.

Elegy For Robert Jebb

The local newspaper
throws at me:
<u>Dead at 46.</u>

The paleness, the curious
long nose, the dart of eye,
the soft sweater look, the cool
asking voice haunts the sleep
out of me.

Many years in writing, pulling
together, publishing his novel,
MIRAGES. Few copies sold.
Despondent then, he moved on,
left us.

Kudos flowing from elsewhere.
An old story ... no recognition
at home, without honour
until today.

I reread the book,
his inscription:
<u>To Esther</u>
<u>with hopes</u>
<u>for better communication</u>
<u>for all of us</u>

...the praying man

*b*ut who am I to confound?

like the stick-head of a mantis
he positioned to pray,
his head bent low, gently, grace-
fully touching the wood in the pew
ahead.

Thoughts we shall not know, really;
for peace in heart to a dying woman;
relief in freedom to go to Magdalene;
early brought-to-believe doctrines
insinuating fear; or his presence
with others to give self-meaning;
perhaps it was loneliness; family shine;
forgiveness; or simply nothing, unfettered.

I'm tough o Lord.

Morning

Wake up trying out for the day
at a four hour breakfast.
It all came from the center;
need for food, brain, high hour
of exchange, hug.
Each focus stayed cool to stay;
waiting, building, time to evap-
orate, maybe end, maybe never.

-- for Michael

Texas Afternoon

Sitting on a bench on a path
next to the Colorado River
where runners run, I remember
again the homeless young man
pushing a steel shopping cart
piled high with his belongings.
I thought, another ripple on the river...
He stopped, dug into the pile
of things and handed over to me
a beautiful apple.
I turned away, shook my head.
He shook, too, and followed the river.
This happening never quite leaves me.

--for Richard
--for Jergen

Elizabeth

*T*his is my cry for help:
<u>Why must you die;</u>

> Elizabeth Morris. Killed instantly
> on Maine turnpike, summer, 1993. A
> piece of bridge abutment or loose pot-
> hole fell or was thrown from above,
> crashing onto her car's windshield.

I still seek your eyes,
nerved to place them

I recognize the dream; watching,
feeling desperate in longing

to place the severed neck, the eyes,
the face, the voice to comfort me.

With Faith and Truth secure,
your hymn holds.

A Canvas
mixed media...still fresh

*n*ot finished,
hold it up front,
stretch the eye,
see in the dusk
a heavy hung tunnel of clouds
scalloped in silver.
Is it a face? God's grace?
Coming night?
Waiting chair. Phone:
an up-down-hug caressing
the Carolinas voice;
<u>the mockingbirds are sounding
sweet in my backyard.</u> Come close.

Listening: laughter in reply
stretch the eye,
etch the glow of a cranberry
glass bowl with 20 yellow daffodils,
gold trumpet-horn daffodils
carolling from New Hampshire earth.
<u>Come close.</u>

Lovers

It is almost winter
to quickly bring us together

she cries use me, use my love
for nights ahead by the fire

santolina gathered, hangs in the hole
of my sweater. Tansy awaits her
come quickly

quickly come. It's what they haven't found
barks at the soul

Legs

The romance has been going on a long time.
As of puppets, legs hang loose from all sorts
of people. All sorts of time. From a
high-up window of my home I watch legs.
I watch, watch with urgency. Fascinated.
They are unaware of me.

I long for a closer look. Social? Sexual?
Mindful? I want to know who belongs to these
legs? The chap in green-striped running shorts
and orange T-shirt. The older woman with white
hair tied back. Is she as strong willed as her
stride? The small girl whose legs turn every
which way in cavort. The dressed-up old man's
legs being pulled by a scrappy poodle on leash.
Teenagers skipping, breaking from holding hands.
Pushcart pushing legs in jeans . . . on and on
they come and go.

All heading in for the Crossover street.

Time Waits Out Time

The lightened bone mass
breaks upon itself,
the limb hangs weakened,
it is positioned
to remembering

>   deep, deep stone steps down
>   Roman wine cellar

>   Christmas Eve run-run
>   wild - black limousine

>   steep steps to friend's house
>   the tall trees waving

>   push for that last climb
>   on - on the Great Wall

>   climb rise to watch moon
>   slide behind the great
>   Monadnock Mountain

>   whirling dance alone
>   cast contemplating

The Narcissus Eye

In the garden the hawthorn tree
blooms again. My eyes are in
longing, the right one for the left.

The surgeon's sword was skilled.
The blood did run; tears overran
the cheek shadowed in full flower.

In the garden apple blossoms waffed
through my hair. Spirited anew,
the old one, my right eye, brightens
in the Garden of the Good.

Home Free

After the poetry reading

the fog along the coast
had seduced my mind into
a feathering of sleep.
The subliminal sex from the poet's
work lighted my dream world
with delight. Intimacies floated;
faces, places, parts of bodies,
but mostly talk; orchestration
of spirits. Then the ordination
tough in force holding us together.
Wings of birds rolled in, close,
nipping my feet and head. Frightened,
I shrieked! Awake, turning, turning
to the dawn, found I was slipping
from the bed. Detached from the dream
hysterics I felt a mounting trans-
figuration. A strong, sinewy eyeball
pushed me back ... easy to find
him here; true love; the genesis
of our sons; an honest thinking
toward life.
His years-long-dead bones and eyes
held me steadfast.

Friendship

It is never to be lonely. Like the
wild white carrot top heads up
among strong stemmed zinnias!
Full of balances and dangers.
Bones do not recognize any meanness,
no little hills of unlove.
Surprise encounter; the sprocket wheels
of the wheelchair mesh with ease,
and without sound.

It is to know the morning.
Among the flowers of a rooftop garden,
a tender white winged butterfly
flutters in out of nowhere, alights,
dips, brushes one to one, and goes its way.

*You loved **Unflappable Women**...*
Be sure to read
Grandmother's **Q**uilt
also by Esther Buffler

Hardcover
128 Pages
$12.95
I.S.B.N. 0-8233-0444-2

Golden Quill Press
Manchester Center, Vermont
Publishers Since 1902

Call 1-800-258-1505 To Order
Or request it at your favorite bookstore